...IT'S A BIRD...
IT'S A PLANE...
IT'S A CROCK!

by

Bill Rechin and Don Wilder

FAWCETT GOLD MEDAL • NEW YORK

Published by Fawcett Gold Medal Books, a unit of
CBS Publications, the Educational and Profes-
sional Publishing Division of CBS, Inc.

ISBN 0–449–14480–1

Printed in the United States of America

First Fawcett Gold Medal Edition: July 1982
10 9 8 7 6 5 4 3 2 1

READY... ...AIM...

STOP!..YOU'RE SUPPOSED TO FEED ME BREAKFAST FIRST!

YOU'RE RIGHT, SCHMEESE.

WHO SAYS CROCK HAS NO HEART?

Bill Rechin

LOAD TWO EGGS IN FRONT OF THE CANNONBALL.

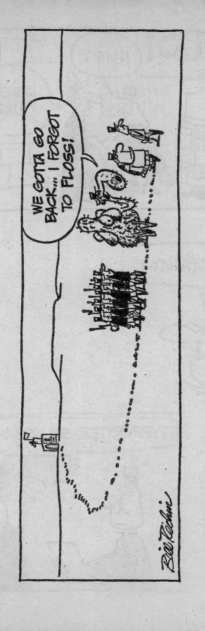

S
P
L
A
T!

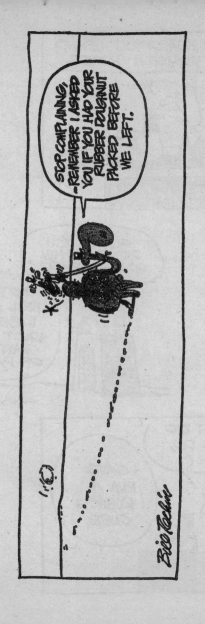

OH MIGHTY NEBUKANEZZER, ...I GOT PROBLEMS YOU **WON'T** BELIEVE.

MY LIFE IS **NOTHING** BUT DRINK AND **WILD WOMEN.**

SKIP THE **GOOD PART** AND GET ON WITH THE PROBLEMS.

Bill Rechin

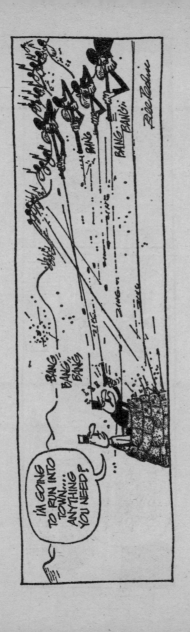

OPEN THE GATE!...IT'S THE LONG-LOST SEYMOUR.

SEYMOUR...YOU'VE BEEN MISSING SIX MONTHS... ...WHAT HAPPENED?

I STOPPED FOR A SECOND AND THEY BUILT A FAST-FOOD RESTAURANT ON TOP OF ME.

WHY DID YOU DO THAT TO A LITTLE DAISY, SIR?

DID YOU EVER TRY DOING IT TO AN OAK TREE?

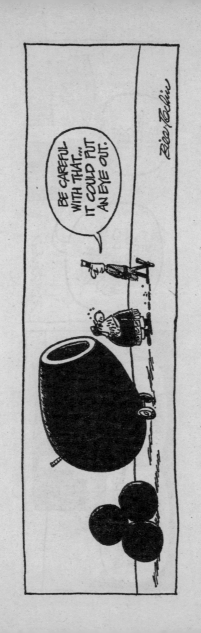

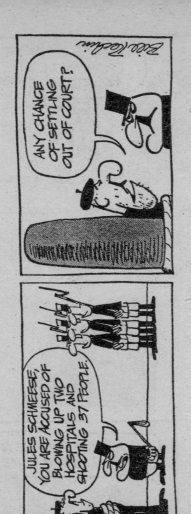

Bill Rechin

Bill Rechin

OH MIGHTY NEBUKANEZZER, ...I NEED YOUR EXALTED ADVICE

HOW CAN I SPICE UP MY LOVE LIFE?

DO I LOOK LIKE A KINKY STONEHENGE?

Bill Rechin

WE GOT HALF AN HOUR BEFORE THE BATTLE. ...ANYBODY GOT ANY LAST-MINUTE SUGGESTIONS?

LET'S HAVE A "TAILGATE PARTY"